D0710541

DISCARD

TRADITIONS AND CELEBRATIONS

EID AL-ADHA

by Mariam Mohamed

PEBBLE
a capstone imprint

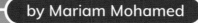

002000612198

Published by Pebble, an imprint of Capstone.
1710 Roe Crest Drive
North Mankato, Minnesota 56003
capstonepub.com

Library of Congress Cataloging-in-Publication Data
Names: Mohamed, Mariam, author.
Title: Eid al-Adha / Mariam Mohamed.
Description: North Mankato, Minnesota : Pebble Explore is published by Pebble, an imprint of Capstone, 2022. | Series: Traditions & celebrations | Includes bibliographical references and index. | Audience: Ages 5-8 | Audience: Grades K-1 | Summary: "Eid al-Adha is about celebrating! It is a Muslim festival remembering the sacrifice Ibrahim was willing to make. People mark the festival with prayer, visiting family, and gifts. Some people sacrifice an animal and share the meat with their community. Readers will discover how a shared holiday can have multiple traditions and be celebrated in all sorts of ways"—Provided by publisher.
Identifiers: LCCN 2021012623 (print) | LCCN 2021012624 (ebook) | ISBN 9781663908353 (hardcover) | ISBN 9781663920904 (paperback) | ISBN 9781663908322 (pdf) | ISBN 9781663908346 (kindle edition)
Subjects: LCSH: ʿĪd al-Aḍḥā—Juvenile literature. | Fasts and feasts—Islam—Juvenile literature. | Islam—Juvenile literature.
Classification: LCC BP186.6 .M64 2022 (print) | LCC BP186.6 (ebook) | DDC 297—dc23
LC record available at https://lccn.loc.gov/2021012623
LC ebook record available at https://lccn.loc.gov/2021012624

Image Credits
Alamy: Charles O. Cecil, 20, Hanan Isachar, 26, Philip Game, 25; AP Images: Nabil al-Jurani, 5, 23; Getty Images: Anadolu Agency/Contributor, 12, 19, Charlotte Observer/Contributor, 13, Hindustan Times/Contributor, 11, Robert Nickelsberg/Contributor, 24, The Washington Post/Contributor, 18; Newscom: ZUMA Press/Narayan Maharjan, 29; Shutterstock; all_about_people, 28, Creativa Images, 1, Fevziie, 14, FOTOKITA, 7, JOAT, Cover, Mama Belle and the kids, 21, Muhd Imran Ismail, 10, Nurlan Mammadzada, 8, Odua Images, 17, Rowr, 22

Artistic elements: Shutterstock: Rafal Kulik

Editorial Credits
Editor: Erika L. Shores; Designer: Dina Her; Media Researcher: Jo Miller; Production Specialist: Tori Abraham

All internet sites appearing in back matter were available and accurate when this book was sent to press.

Printed and bound in the USA. 004270

TABLE OF CONTENTS

Words in **bold** are in the glossary.

THE TWO EIDS

A family is baking fresh Eid cookies. Tomorrow is Eid al-Adha. Eid means festival. **Muslims** celebrate two Eids. They are known as Eid al-Adha and Eid al-Fitr. Eid al-Adha is the **holier** festival of the two Eids.

Muslims around the world celebrate Eid al-Adha every year. The holiday **honors** the story of **Prophet Ibrahim**. The story goes that Ibrahim was willing to sacrifice, or give up, his son to Allah (God). Allah rewarded him by saving his son and sacrificing an animal instead.

THE MONTH OF DHUL HIJJA

Muslims use a **lunar** calendar. It has 354 days. Eid al-Adha takes place on the 10th day of the last month. This is known as the month of Dhul Hijja. It happens during summer.

Crescent moons are important in the religion of **Islam**. Muslims use the crescent moon to tell them when Eid will be. When the new moon comes out, it means Eid al-Adha will begin in 10 days. The date of Eid al-Adha changes every year.

The Kaaba in Mecca

HAJJ

Several days before the holiday, millions of Muslims go to the cities of Mecca and Mina. They perform **Hajj** there. Hajj begins on the eighth day in the month of Dhul Hijja. All Muslims should do Hajj once in their lives if they are able.

Mecca and Mina are in the country of Saudi Arabia. Muslims from around the world go to Mecca to visit the Kaaba, or House of Allah. This is why Mecca is the most important city for Muslims. It is the holy land.

WUDHU

Prayer is an important part of Islam. Muslims get ready for prayer by performing wudhu. Wudhu means to wash in a special way. All Muslims need to wash their hands, arms, mouth, nose, face, ears, neck, head, and feet. People must be very clean to join in any Eid prayer.

Wearing clean clothes is also important. In order to pray, clothes can't have any dirt or stains. Muslims must always look and smell their best when praying.

EID PRAYER

If you can't perform Hajj, don't worry! People can celebrate by going to the **mosque** in the morning for the Eid prayer. They remember to wear their best clean clothes.

Inside a mosque

Several people come together to take part in the Eid prayer. It can be done inside a mosque or outside on a field. Everyone stands shoulder to shoulder when praying.

MAKING DUA

Making dua in Islam means to talk to Allah. Muslims make dua by raising their hands up and asking Allah for favors. Duas can also be used to ask to be forgiven. Dua can be made anytime and anywhere.

After the Eid prayer is done, Muslims can make dua and ask Allah for anything. Dua can be done quietly. It can also be said out loud for others to hear. When someone makes dua for you, you say "Ameen."

THE QURAN

On the day of Eid, Muslims read the Quran. The Quran is the holy book for Muslims. Muslims pray five times a day and read the Quran during prayer. It can also be read at other times.

The words of the Quran are written in Arabic. Many Muslims learn to read and write in Arabic.

Reading the Quran

CHARITY

Taking care of others is an important part of Eid. After the Eid prayer is done, Muslim families cook an animal and have a feast.

The animal is split into three parts. This is known as **Qurbani**. One part of the animal is given to the poor. Another part is given to your family at home. The last part is saved to be shared with your neighbors or relatives.

Sometimes mosques will also make meals for those celebrating the holiday. Some Muslim families may also give money to a **charity**.

BEING KIND MATTERS

Muslims are to show kindness to others whenever they can. There are many ways to do acts of kindness. On Eid Day, Muslim children offer to clean up the mosques after a gathering. Some might offer to share their new toys or money with someone in need.

Children sweep the floor in a mosque.

A child might ask a friend over for a meal. Some might send cards to special people. Even a smile can cheer someone up. No act of kindness is too small.

PREPARING FOR EID

The week before Eid, many people make it a **tradition** to decorate their homes. People use glittered crescent moons and star shapes. Some might hang up string lights. They cut out paper animals to hang up.

Baking Eid cookies is another
tradition Muslim families enjoy. Some
children love to help put together
goodie bags for their Eid guests.
Getting ready for the holiday is
very exciting!

EID PARTIES

Some people throw Eid parties. Relatives and friends come over, and they all celebrate together. They make a big meal and share stories with each other. People eat cakes, cookies, and lots of other sweets.

Eid picnics are also fun. Sometimes people go to a popular restaurant with their loved ones. There are many ways to celebrate Eid.

EIDI

Sometimes grown-ups give children money on Eid day. Children sometimes give sweets or gifts to each other. This is known as Eidi. Eidi is a gift given on Eid day. But Eid is not only about money and gifts. It is a special day to show you care about other people.

Some people make Eid Mubarak cards for their loved ones. Eid Mubarak means "Blessed Feast" or "Blessed Festival." Making cards to wish people Eid Mubarak is a nice thing to do, and people love to receive them.

Another way to show people you care is to call them. You can call and say, "As-salamu alaykum!" Muslims usually greet each other with this. It means "Peace be upon you!"

Eid is a special time of the year for all Muslims. It is celebrated around the world. Everyone celebrates Eid in their own special way. The most important thing on this day is to show kindness to all.

GLOSSARY

charity (CHAYR-uh-tee)—a group that raises money to help people in need

crescent (KRE-suhnt)—the shape of the visible part of the moon when it is less than half full

Hajj (HAJ)—the journey every Muslim should make to the holy land at least once in their lifetime

holy (HOH-lee)—connected to a god or a religion

honor (ON-ur)—to give praise or show respect

Islam (ISS-luhm)—the religion of Muslims, based on the teachings of the Prophet Muhammad

lunar (LOO-nur)—having to do with the moon

mosque (MOSK)—a place of worship for Muslims

Muslim (MUHZ-luhm)—a follower of the religion of Islam; Muslims believe in one God, Allah, and that Muhammad is his prophet

Prophet Ibrahim (PROF-it EE-bruh-heem)—a messenger for Allah (God); Ibrahim is also called Abraham

Qurbani (KOOR-baa-nee)—to sacrifice, or to give up, an animal, such as a sheep, goat, or camel on Eid day

tradition (truh-DISH-uhn)—a custom, idea, or belief passed down through time

READ MORE

Currie-McGhee, L.K. *Muslim in America*. San Diego, CA: ReferencePoint Press, Inc., 2021.

Oxley, Jennifer and Billy Aronson. *Peg + Cat: The Eid al-Adha Adventure*. Somerville, MA: Candlewick Entertainment, 2018.

Vallepur, Shalini. *Eid al-Adha*. United Kingdom: BookLife Publishing, 2019.

INTERNET SITES

Eid al-Adha Facts for Kids
kids.kiddle.co/Eid_al-Adha

Hajj and Eid ul Adha for Kids
multiculturalkidblogs.com/2015/09/09/hajj-eid-ul-adha-kids/

Learn All about the Muslim Festival Eid al-Adha
cbc.ca/kidscbc2/the-feed/learn-all-about-the-muslim-festival-eid-al-adha

INDEX